THE FOURTH CANDLE

THE FOURTH CANDLE

Messages for Advent, Christmas, and Epiphany

BY PER LØNNING

Translated by O. G. Malmin

AUGSBURG PUBLISHING HOUSE
MINNEAPOLIS, MINNESOTA

THE FOURTH CANDLE
Sermons from Advent to Epiphany
Copyright © 1970 by Augsburg Publishing House
All rights reserved
Library of Congress Catalog Card No. 76-121963

This volume is a translation of *Det Fjerde Lys* published in 1965 by Land og Kirke, Oslo, Norway.

Scripture quotations are from the Revised Standard Version of the Bible, copyright 1946 and 1952 by the Division of Christian Education of the National Council of Churches.

Hymns from the *Service Book and Hymnal* are used by permission of the Commission on the Liturgy and the Hymnal. Stanzas from *The Lutheran Hymnary* are identified with the initials LH.

MANUFACTURED IN THE UNITED STATES OF AMERICA

Contents

Translator's Preface 9

Today ... in Your Ears .... Luke 4:16-22   11
FIRST SUNDAY IN ADVENT

Lift Your Heads! .... Luke 21:25-36   21
SECOND SUNDAY IN ADVENT

At the Border Station .... Matthew 11:11-15   29
THIRD SUNDAY IN ADVENT

Is It True? .... John 5:31-40   39
FOURTH SUNDAY IN ADVENT

Happiness for Everyone .... Luke 2:10   49
CHRISTMAS MESSAGE TO CHILDREN

God Gave His Son .... Luke 2:1-14   57
CHRISTMAS DAY

Christmas in Our Sort of World   Matthew 23:34-39   65
ST. STEPHEN'S DAY

Heaven's Melody Is Not Silenced .. Luke 1:68-75   73
SUNDAY AFTER CHRISTMAS

In Your Hand .... Psalm 31:14-16   81
NEW YEAR'S EVE

Fruit .... Luke 13:6-9   91
NEW YEAR'S DAY

Many Stars—And One Star ...... Matthew 2:1-12   101
EPIPHANY

7

Translator's Preface

These sermons come from the pen of one of Norway's foremost churchmen, the Rt. Rev. Dr. Per Lønning, bishop of the newly-created diocese of Borg, in the southern part of Norway. Elevated to the episcopacy at the age of 40, Lønning is the youngest bishop Norway has had since the early part of the nineteenth century.

Long before he became bishop, Lønning's name was known throughout the land of Norway. Pastor, preacher, scholar, statesman—he had acquired a well-deserved reputation as all four. The selection of sermons in this volume speaks to the wideness of his popularity as a preacher.

It is never easy to answer the question, "What makes a sermon great?" As far as Lønning's preaching is concerned, several things may be said without fear of contradiction. First, his preaching is evangelical. It is the gospel of Christ coming into the world as God's redeeming gift to men. Certainly, Advent, Christmas, and Epiphany would have little meaning without that as the central emphasis.

Next, one is captivated by the simplicity of his preaching. Lønning knows the secret of being profoundly simple, or shall we say simply profound. Never does the exegetical and dogmatic study which preceded the delivery of the sermon intrude itself. One may say that his preaching is simple, for as one reads these sermons, one is carried into the depths of God's revelation, scarcely knowing by what route he got there.

Finally, his preaching is fresh and contemporary. In choice of words and in use of illustrations, his language is the language of today. The translator discovered that it was not difficult to make his contemporary illustrations speak American instead of Norwegian.

It is our hope that Lønning will speak to present-day America through this volume as eloquently as he did in his earlier volume, *Pathways of the Passion,* and as he did to his own countrymen in both volumes.

O. G. MALMIN

TODAY ... IN YOUR EARS

Luke 4:16-22   FIRST SUNDAY IN ADVENT

Let us live, Lord, by your Word, today and every day!
Let the new church year which begins today be a good
year, a year in which your Word brings release to our
hearts. Amen.

"Today this scripture has been fulfilled in your
hearing." That is the way we read the text. But
that is not, strictly speaking, what Jesus said. An
older and more accurate translation of the original Greek is : "Today this scripture has been fulfilled *in your ears.*" It would be still more accurate
to say, *"for your ears."*

However we translate it, there is something
peculiar here. We would expect Jesus to say,
"Today this scripture has been fulfilled *in your*
eyes." Only when we have actually *seen* something can we be certain that it is so.

11

Hearing and Seeing

The fact that we have *heard* something is no proof that it is so. Suppose that I am aware of an ancient saying that some day a king shall appear who will set the human race free. Then one day someone stands before me and says, "Now the saying has been fulfilled. Here I stand. Through these words you have heard what the whole thing means."

What good does it do me that the saying has been fulfilled in my ears, that someone *says* that he fulfills it? I must use my eyes. I need to study the one who stands there. Can I see any signs which testify to the truth of what he says? Does he look the way I think a king ought to look? Is there any sign that he has done such great things that I can know with absolute certainty that he can help me as he says he can? Or is his statement only words?

The gospel is only words, we say. Jesus himself said, "Blessed are those who have not seen and yet believe." The truth is that there is nothing to see, nothing to make the whole thing simple and straightforward, nothing to help us accept the Word which seeks our trust and obedience.

We see the meaning of this in what transpired after the events of our text. Everything seemed so wonderful; everyone seemed so friendly. "And all spoke well of him, and wondered at the gracious words which proceeded out of his mouth; and they said, 'Is not this Joseph's son?' "

But then Jesus continued, "Doubtless you will quote to me this proverb, 'Physician, heal thyself; what we have heard you did at Capernaum, do here also in your own country,' " Then he went on, "Truly, I say to you, no prophet is acceptable in his own country." He reminded them that the prophets Elijah and Elisha were sent to foreigners. And the people became so furious with Jesus that they threw him out of the city and wanted to hurl him over a precipice.

This is not the only time we learn of people demanding signs and wonders of Jesus. They say, "Give us absolute evidence, then we will accept you. But do not expect us to venture out on thin ice; do not expect that we will take a leap into the dark." Their motto is "Safety first!"

The Purpose of the Miracles

But didn't Jesus at times give proofs? Even though he sometimes refused, wanting to influence people without the "safety" of miracles, we cannot overlook the fact that he did perform many wonderful works, signs and miracles which people saw. Doesn't that mean that his words were fulfilled before their *eyes?*

Yes, that is true, but that was not the purpose

of his miracles. After the miraculous feeding in the wilderness, he fled from the crowd when they wanted to seize him and make him king by force. We likewise remember the temptation in the wilderness, when he said no to all the proposals of the enemy that he use his divine power to take a shortcut to the royal throne. And in the end his great works were used against him: "He saved others; let him save himself."

I wonder if we actually would have received any help in our spiritual problems if we had lived in Jesus' day and had been eyewitnesses to what happened. I doubt it. I do not come to have faith in a miracle and in the one who performs it merely by standing as an astonished witness. There is a question which I must answer in my heart. There is a conviction which I must consciously embrace and make my own.

About three hundred years ago something remarkable took place in a cloister in France. A young girl with an eye disease was healed when she touched a relic which was supposed to be a piece of Jesus' crown of thorns. The supposed miracle took place among the Jansenists, a group of Christians close to the Reformation, who were being persecuted by the Jesuits and by the ruler of the land. Now, the Jansenists thought, God had given proof that they were in the right and had the special protection of heaven! But what of the Jesuits? They agreed that God had surely performed a miracle. But, they maintained, he had done it to call a halt to those horrible Jansenists and turn them to better thoughts. The miracle, they said, was a warning.

I mention this episode to show how difficult it is to get wisdom from a miracle. It all depends on the interpretation of the miracle, and the interpretation is colored by the attitude of the interpreter. Either *I* speak the last word, or I permit myself to listen to some voice that speaks to me. The picture cannot speak until words give it meaning.

Jesus does not want our opinions, he wants our hearts. He did not come into the world with a new world view but with a new love. He loved his neighbor more than himself, his God more than the joys that do not last. His desire was to *be* good rather than to *have it* good.

That is why he does not come to us with proof for our eyes. He speaks to us through our ears, explaining life to us, telling us of God's promises, helping us to faith and trust and surrender. The motto is not "Safety first!" It is, "Speak, Lord, for your servant hears."

Seeing and Believing

Of course there is a great deal to *see* also. The multitude had many things to see. They could

see all those wonderful works the Gospel calls
signs, and which are first and foremost picture
language, illustrations for the words Jesus speaks.

And they could see him, this poor rabbi from
Nazareth. To them he looked not a bit more remarkable than other rabbis they had seen. Quite
the contrary. Most of the rabbis had some sort of
diploma to show that they had had training.
Jesus did not even have that. What they saw was
a person who shared with the rest of them everyday life and ordinary conditions, one who loved
to seek out the sick and those who carried heavy
burdens in order that he might give them rest.

What did this mean? The Word gave the answer. He was the Word, which "became flesh and
dwelt among us, full of grace and truth." Who,
then, *saw?* Only the one who first listened and
accepted in his heart what he had heard. For him
everything he had seen became clear. It appeared
in a new light and became great and wonderful
above all else. This was heaven on earth: God had
come to us to share in our lives. We are no longer
lost and lonely, because he is with us.

Salvation is not something invisible or ethereal
or off somewhere in the heavens. The God who
came down and shared our flesh and blood—even
if the eye could not interpret what it saw—is visible in the same way today. The church, the body
of Christ, is visible, with all its faults and fail-

ings. The means of grace are visible: the baptismal water, the bread and the wine which we receive in Communion.

Christ the man speaks to the entire man. But the entryway to the soul is still the ear. It is the Word which opens the way, which explains and clarifies. It is not by accident that the evangelist calls Jesus the Word. We do not need ritual to create the right emotions or proofs to convince us. We need surrender and faith in him who speaks, childlike certainty that all God's promises are kept.

"The Acceptable Year of the Lord"

It is from this perspective that we, on this First Sunday in Advent, preach on the Word which bids us to "proclaim the acceptable year of the Lord." This "acceptable year" begins today. And it will greet us every Sunday as we gather in the house of God to sing our thanks for the great wonder which again and again is fulfilled in our ears—the wonder of the incarnation, the wonder of God coming to us. There is an Immanuel—God with us.

To demand more than that is to demand less. The Word demands surrender, and to sneak past surrender is the sure way to sneak past the blessing which the Word reveals. For how shall my

thought, my understanding, my wisdom be able
to know God when he appears; how can I examine his credentials? But "my sheep hear my voice"
—that voice goes from the ear to the heart. It can
incite our stubborn minds to wonder and praise,
and create in us certainty and security.

The miracle above all miracles is that this voice
speaks to us, reaches us, shows us who we are and
what our hope of salvation is: that God is a God
who comes down to us, who reaches out to the
poor in spirit and offers them his hand. In comparison with that miracle, all the miracles which
the eye can see become nothing.

"The Spirit of the Lord is upon me, because he
has anointed me to preach good news to the poor.
He has sent me to proclaim release to the captives
and recovering of sight to the blind, to set at liberty those who are oppressed, to proclaim the
acceptable year of the Lord."

How many there are who today testify, both in
the church militant here on earth and in the
church triumphant before the throne of God, that
this is the truth, that this has been fulfilled for
us in our ears and in our lives. We have been
loosed from our chains; we have found a sight
which has put an end to our blindness. We have
found everything as he promised it.

It doesn't matter that we have no proofs to present which the world will accept, that we can't

convince anyone through scholarly analysis. He is the one who created meaningfulness out of meaninglessness in my life and made me see all things in a new light. "One thing I know, that though I was blind, now I see." Amen.

LIFT YOUR HEADS!

Luke 21:25-26   SECOND SUNDAY IN ADVENT

Lord, you know everything which burdens and op-
presses us. You know that even on this festive day, when
we are supposed to be people of great importance, we
feel small and insignificant. Help us all, young and old,
to listen to your voice. Steel us, make us strong, so that
we may be able to overcome the power of despondency.
Help us to lift our heads and go courageously out to
meet you. Amen.

Congratulations and best wishes to confirmands
and parents on this day! For all of us it is a festival day. For the young people and their families it
is a milepost. It is both right and proper to make
it a day of rejoicing and happiness in the family
circle, and it is fitting that we do so here in God's
house. Today's Gospel makes a mighty contribu-
tion toward making this day what it should be.

Am I joking? Here we are told that heaven and
earth shall pass away; that men shall faint with

fear and foreboding of what is coming on the world; that the powers of the heavens will be shaken; that someone will appear in a cloud with power and great glory to call us to judgment and accounting. Surely it would take less than that to destroy a festival atmosphere!

Strength and Courage for the Future

I can well imagine that some of you had a feeling of protest when you heard me read this text. I hope so. If not, it must mean that you are exceedingly pious or that you were not paying attention—probably the latter.

Your protest might be something like this: Isn't there enough in today's world to rob us of our courage? We live in a difficult and insecure time. What we all need—and not least these attractive young confirmands who must find their future—is balance and courage to go ahead. The church should not steal from them their joy in the future; it should give them faith in tomorrow, faith in progress, faith that life matters.

That is exactly right. The church's task is to give people faith; its errand is to instill in them power and stability. The Master makes that perfectly clear. "Look up and raise your heads," he says in our text. It is not his intention to crush us under more sorrows and anxieties.

Jesus is here to give us strength and courage—for tomorrow and for an uncertain future. But there are two ways of instilling courage. You can slap someone on the back and encourage him with "There, there, don't take it so hard; you will soon see that it is not as bad as it seems." A person who is eloquent and knows psychology can make a mouse believe it can swallow a rattlesnake. But the mouse probably doesn't enjoy the results of that kind of courage!

The courage which minimizes danger and makes you believe that you can conquer the world by your own strength is useless. You young people are not strong if you sally forth into the world believing that life is harmless, that you yourself will be able to solve all the difficulties you meet, and that success is yours for the taking. The one who is strong understands the seriousness of life, recognizes its pitfalls, and knows how to surmount them.

Only two kinds of people feel secure. There are those who see less and therefore do not understand the risks of life. And there are those who see more, who see not only the threat but also God's throne. They will always find the right way out.

"Heaven and earth will pass away," says Jesus. He doesn't say it to frighten us nor to discourage us from taking seriously the world and the life God has given us. As long as the world stands, and as long as we find ourselves here on earth and not somewhere out in space, we must take it for granted that this is God's will for us.

At times people throw away their spades and kettles because they are convinced that Jesus is coming again tomorrow. That is the worst kind of irresponsibility. The sects and sensation-preachers who advertise in big headlines the exact time Jesus will come again are sinning against his words, that no one knows or can know the day or the hour. Martin Luther was right when he said that even if he knew that the world would be destroyed tomorrow, he would still go out in his garden and plant an apple tree today.

When God keeps me here, it is because he wants me here. He has given me strength and ability in order that I may employ them for useful purposes. You young people have sensible and worthy goals: education, work, love, marriage. And everything you will be able to contribute to the life around you—furthering peace, liberty, and the welfare of your fellow man—is all in accord with the mind of the Creator. You can enter the day which awaits you with assurance and faith.

The Basis of Faith

Our faith must rest on an unshakable foundation. It must be far more than a trust in chance or a conviction that everything will turn out well. That is why Jesus reminds us that nothing we see is eternal: "Heaven and earth will pass away, but my words will not pass away." If we are to avoid setting up false standards and building our lives on faulty premises, we must *know* the truth and *choose* the truth.

Man is created with an inborn need to find something which endures, something unchangeable, something that will not pass away. Many people never get beyond substitutes: money, position, power, beauty, things temporal. These things have their place if we do not make them *the* objects of life. The one who lives for this world and its treasures will be swallowed up in them.

Sooner or later all this will disappear, and I will have to say farewell to it. What, then, can I count on? No one knows what will happen to the planet on which we live—whether it will continue to be habitable a few million more years, or whether it will disappear in a man-made or cosmic catastrophe.

Let us hope and pray and work to make life on earth as good and rich and beautiful as we can. Let us do everything we can to make conditions of life as good as possible for those who come after us. As for the rest, let us leave the future in God's hand!

Science tells us that sooner or later life as we know it will no longer exist. Endless generations may come and go before that takes place, or it may come tomorrow. No one knows. What we do know is that in a hundred years—shall we say a hundred and fifty to be on the safe side?—none of us will be here. As far as we are concerned, the world will then have disappeared and if it continues to exist for our grandchildren and their grandchildren, that will mean nothing to us. Heaven and earth will have passed away—for us.

But if we are to keep up our courage, should we not close our minds to such disturbing thoughts? If we do, ours will be a poor sort of courage indeed! We need the ability to look straight at the facts and square our shoulders and lift our heads. Christianity did not invent the end of the world; it only wants to tear us away from a false sense of security and plant us firmly on what is genuine. Christianity tells us that we will not attain fearlessness by closing our eyes, but by opening them.

It is not death which is coming, nor the end of the world, nor catastrophes, nor accidents, nor frustrations. When we try to analyze the signs of the times, it seems that these are what we have to fear. But the Word of God says that it is our Lord Jesus Christ who is coming. When our earthly kingdoms and their glory disappear, we will learn that there is one kingdom that endures.

That Which Changes Not

That kingdom was planted in our world when the Son of God shared our life and our death and won a victory which we share. As surely as we belong to him, we are citizens of the kingdom which is eternal. His word and promises are unchanging. When we some day see him face to face—he, not we, knows when—there will be joy and glory like nothing we have ever known. If we live in such an expectation, we can surely lift our heads!

> Fighting, we shall be victorious
> By the Blood of Christ our Lord;
> On our foreheads, bright and glorious,
> Shines the witness of his word;
> Spear and shield on battlefield,
> His great Name; we cannot yield.
>
> (SBH 556, stanza 3)

A look into the future should make me gloriously happy. I know that my life here will continue exactly as long as God decrees, and that he will assign me just those duties he has prepared for me. And all the seed I sow here on earth I will see again as flowers in God's garden.

Even though the world seems to close in on me and place obstacles in my path; even though adversity and frustration and despondency try to build a wall which obscures my vision; even though everything here on earth which gives me happiness withers and fades and disappears, one thing remains—the joy of all joys, Jesus Christ.

Some day I shall meet him. I do not know how; that is for him to decide. I simply say with the hymn writer:

> The King shall come when morning dawns,
> And light and beauty brings:
> Hail, Christ the Lord! Thy people pray,
> Come quickly, King of kings.
>
> (SBH 10, stanza 5)

This is the perspective for youth of all ages. Certainly there is no one who understands and feels more strongly than you young people what it is to await a *new* heaven and a *new* earth. Let us till our old earth with faithfulness and affection, but let us never become so immersed in it that we are swallowed up by the very furrow we dig!

Our eyes must always be turned toward that which is new, toward him who is to come, the Renewer. Let us walk through life with heads lifted. Ahead of us, like the morning sky, gleams the new and great day, the day of Jesus Christ. Amen.

AT THE BORDER STATION

Matthew 11:11-15   THIRD SUNDAY IN ADVENT

*Our Lord and our King, we thank you for the open
door that you have set before us. Help us to enter it.
Amen.*

To John had been entrusted a task that is not
popular in our day. John is God's border guard.

We live in an age which is anxious to do away
with borders and boundaries. We have the United
Nations, free trade treaties, common markets, One
World movements. We have means of communi-
cation that have done away with distance and
have made everyone in the whole world neighbors. We have discovered the worth of foreign
cultures. Race discrimination is decreasing. We
are world citizens who place our emphasis on
what unites people and disregard what separates
them.

In such a world the voice of John seems strange, even frightening. Although his message has nothing to do with cooperation among nations and the well-meant efforts to break down the world's fences, John is the messenger of a kingdom which resists all efforts at compromise, a kingdom which has definite borders and guards them.

It is not on his own initiative that this stern border guard has taken up his position. The King has placed him there. In our text it is as though the King looks out of a window in his palace and rests his eyes gratefully on the guard at the palace gate. "Among those born of women," he says, "there has risen no one greater than John the Baptist." Strong words, certainly! Perhaps too strong?

When we were children we perhaps believed that it was better to be a nobody in our own country than to be even the ruler of a foreign land; that it was more wonderful to sit on a barren rock in our own country than to wander among the flower gardens of another country. As we grow older, we discover that this type of nationalism is not only stupid but downright dangerous. To imagine that one's own land and people are more important than others is not patriotism; it is self-glorification.

Is there something similar in the spiritual world—a sort of self-glorification because one is a

Christian? A feeling that the least person who is safely within the Christian borders is better than even the giants who are outside? If that is the case, Christianity does not have much to contribute to peace and understanding in the world.

The Greatness of John

If we look more closely at the "greatness" Jesus is speaking about, we will understand better what sort of kingdom he offers and why that kingdom needs a border guard. John is the greatest person ever born on earth, says Jesus. What is it that makes him so great?

It is not money; that is perfectly clear. Locusts and wild honey to eat and a camel's hair garment to wear do not indicate a very high standard of living even for John's day. It was not position or influence either; John occupied no position of greatness and esteem among the prominent people of his day. Nor was it knowledge or learning; one does not bury those qualities in the sand of the desert. It cannot have been wisdom or shrewdness. Shrewd heads do not end up on a platter, no matter how royal the platter may be.

Was it his courage that made him great, his faithfulness to his convictions despite dangers to his life? Certainly such courage is imposing! But history records thousands who have had equal

courage, so that can hardly be what made John
unique. How about his gentleness—was that so
incomparable? I doubt it. The Gospels picture
him as gruff, sometimes merciless toward his oppo-
nents, and we are told that his faith came near
slipping as he sat in prison. There may well have
been those who excelled him in both meekness
and patience.

What, then, was it? There is one thing that is
completely decisive: his *call*, the position in which
he had been placed. That place is in the presence
of the King.

As John stands at his lonely post he sees the
rays of the morning sun fall on the distant moun-
tain and follows them with his eyes as they come
closer and closer. Soon the sun will have risen,
the earth will be bathed in light. John sees it, he
announces it. No one sees it as plainly as he—because God has showed it to him. No one tells it
as plainly as he—because God places the words
on his lips. His greatness is not due to something
in himself; it lies in the sunrise which is to come,
the sunrise which he is called to announce to the
world. This is the call he has received, and he is
obedient to it.

A New Greatness

That leads us to what Jesus says next: "Yet he
who is least in the kingdom of heaven is greater

than he." "Least in the kingdom of heaven." I wonder if that is not a name Jesus has given himself to emphasize that he has made himself the servant of all.

This also says something about *us*. If we have found a home in his kingdom, we are greater than the patriarchs, greater than the prophets, greater than John. All these stand at our side as servants. We are even greater than Jesus himself, Lord above all lords, who of his own free will made himself the servant of all servants.

So all our reckoning has been turned upside down and we find ourselves in a topsy-turvy world. The treasures of the kingdom belong to the poor, its joys belong to those who mourn, its promises of victory belong to the meek. Blessed are those who are nothing and have nothing; no greatness in themselves, no strength of their own, nothing to lift themselves to the heights to rival God. Let the mountains be made low and the valleys be lifted up, and let a highway for God's majesty be made straight in the desert.

Thus a new sort of greatness is born, contrary to everything the world calls great. It is a greatness which does not consist of the false security of imagining that we are the masters of our own existence. It quite simply consists of being in the presence of the Almighty and accepting each moment as a new and wonderful gift from his hand.

How was this new concept of greatness planted in our world? We discovered what is truly
great when the King of kings descended into our
feeble lives; when he, through suffering and
sacrifice, reached out his hand to us to lead us
through the barriers and fences raised by our
self-made glory. In that way his greatness became
our greatness; in comparison with that anything
significant we attain here on earth is nothing.
What glory can I imagine which can compare
with the glory of standing in the forecourt of the
kingdom of heaven?

A "Converted Kingdom"

This is the new kingdom, the kingdom of Jesus
Christ. The name above the gate is "Conversion"
because it is a "converted kingdom" in which
everything is the opposite of the kingdoms we
ourselves build. A kingdom can continue only as
long as there is consistency between the laws
which control the kingdom and those which are
a part of the individual citizens. The hearts of
king and people must beat in harmony.

That is why the kingdom of heaven needs a
border guard, a John the Baptist stationed at the
entrance gate with the message, "Repent, for the
kingdom of heaven is at hand." Yet he is unlike
any other border guard. The ordinary border

guard welcomes visitors and tourists, but if armed men attempt to take the kingdom by force, he resists.

The "converted" kingdom is different. "From the days of John the Baptist until now the kingdom of heaven has suffered violence, and men of violence take it by force." All tourist traffic is prohibited; you cannot come visiting with the idea that it would be nice to look around and go home with a few souvenirs. John takes care that tourists and curiosity seekers are barred and that only those who are fully armed gain entrance. Only the one who risks himself and his whole existence is welcome.

> Fight the good fight with all thy might,
> Christ is thy strength, and Christ thy right;
> Lay hold on life, and it shall be
> Thy joy and crown eternally.
>
> (SBH 557, stanza 1)

Storming the Gates

Why must the kingdom be taken by force? Does the kingdom itself resist invasion? Does the King prefer that his "blessed little flock" enjoy themselves in safety, no matter what happens to the rest of the world?

No, it is not God's kingdom that offers resistance and refuses to be taken. Resistance comes from a king I myself carry in my heart. That is why force is necessary. I advance boldly to seize truth, to seize life's meaning, to seize the kingdom that beckons. The border guard makes it clear that this is the way it should be. Then, as the fight grows fierce, I discover that *I* am being conquered. The enemy is in *me!* The kingdom is conquered because *it* conquers *me.* I am conquered, "turned about," converted. From the measuring stick of greatness I have hitherto believed in, I am converted to a new concept of greatness, a new kingdom and new laws which burn themselves into my soul and become my precious possessions.

The kingdom is not taken by my shrewdness nor my strength nor my dauntlessness. If these were the weapons with which to storm the gates of heaven and force an entrance, heaven would be a peculiar place! The real conqueror is not I, but "he who is least in the kingdom of heaven." It is Jesus Christ, who made himself so small that he permitted himself to be crushed by my false greatness, and thereby made life and the world and existence truly great for me.

The "Christmas Gate"

He turned everything around so that the gate to greatness stands wide open to all those who, sword in hand, want to seize it by force. The gate stands open to all those who come because they have to, because they must gain entry or perish, because they must find hope, salvation and a solution to life. It is not their heroic effort that opens the gate. The King himself is present and conquers *for* them, *in* them, and *over* them. In his might we win all, and we win because we ourselves are won.

On behalf of the King, John stands guard at the gate of God's kingdom of gentleness and mercy. This is truly the "Christmas gate." John stands guard at a border which only the small and bewildered can cross. The way to the stable and the manger is closed to everything in the world which thinks itself great and proud and splendid.

Christmas, with its defenseless little child at the center, turns all the greatness of the world upside down. Christmas makes everything different. "Unless you turn and become like children, you will never enter the kingdom of heaven."

So Christmas is the great festival of conversion, and it is I who must be converted. Before me looms John, the King's great watchman, and he looks right at me. Amen.

IS IT TRUE?

John 5:31-40   FOURTH SUNDAY IN ADVENT

Lord, we pray that the melody of Christmas may sing its way into our hearts and convince us that the Gospel of joy is true. Amen.

We stand on the threshold of Christmas, ready to step in. Into what? Into a fairy tale, into childhood's lovely dream world where the dark and cold of winter lose their hold on us for a few days?

It is too easy to let Christmas become just that kind of beautiful, fleeting visit to Disneyland. We are unable to connect shepherds and angels and the child in the manger with the world which is ours the rest of the year. If Christmas for us means merely legend and poetry, it has no effect on us the rest of the year—except that we have to tighten our belts for a few weeks in January until our purses recover their health.

If the Christmas gospel is to have any meaning for our lives and our destiny, it must be real and true. If it is not true it can give us no strength. Men may dream and imagine as much as they like; in the end it cannot help them. The only thing that does help is facts, stern realities, events which leave their mark.

It must be a fact that a savior has come down to earth and unlocked for us the gates of heaven. It must be true, as the church proclaims, that God and man have become one in this child in the manger, that God has come down to us so that we can come to him. If this is not fact, there is nothing left but a dream, and nothing has happened to save us. Then we sit alone in the darkness and tell tales about a light that does not exist, or at least does not shine for *us*.

The Impossible Possibility

The church bears testimony to something that has really happened. A savior has really been born; the child who was born has really saved us.

But that is fantastic; it is beyond belief. We cannot comprehend that one person in all history was altogether different from all others. Our minds demand that it be capable of analysis and dissection until it fits into what we already know; it must follow rules with which we are already familiar. A single event, a single person who is altogether different from everything and everyone in our experience—that goes quite beyond our understanding.

How can I know that Jesus is the Son of God? Can anyone prove it? No. In fact, I believe that if the Son of God came down to earth in 1970, it would be impossible for a later generation to find proof of it. We can never prove an event in the same manner that we can prove a mathematical formula. An event which cannot be forecast—in the way, for example, that an eclipse can be predicted—cannot be proved after it is said to have happened.

But certainly concerning events in our world is not based on knowledge of the laws of mathematics or nature. It is based on one of two things: either I myself have witnessed the event, or I have received trustworthy evidence from others who have been witnesses. I know nothing at first hand about events which took place more than nineteen hundred years ago. I must depend on written sources, possibly supplemented by archeological data. Then I will have to use my common sense to judge the trustworthiness of the witnesses and the plausibility of what they say.

If there are a great many witnesses, or if there is reason to consider them especially trustworthy, I will probably accept what they say even if it seems peculiar. However, if the testimony seems weak, I probably will believe the account only if it seems straightforward and plausible. But when the testimony has to do with something absolutely unique, when it concerns something as sensational as the statement that God's Son has come down to us, certainly there will have to be a fantastic witness before I can accept the truth of the account.

A person places himself outside any possibility of discussion if he is satisfied with the simple reasoning of unbelief: this is an impossibility, it *cannot* have happened. That is a preconceived judgment arrived at without taking time to investigate. The witnesses have a right to be heard before one can arrive at a considered judgment.

People Bear Witness

Who, then, are the witnesses? Today's text introduces us to the most important. First we meet John the Baptist. True, he is not the same kind of witness for us as he was for the people who saw and heard him and came under the spell of his enthusiasm.

We know John only through the few brief glimpses the Gospel writers give of him. We cannot prove that these glimpses give us a full and accurate picture of the man. Historians may raise the point that the early church misunderstood him. Although this is unlikely, we cannot dismiss the thought entirely. The account concerning John, the man who foretold the coming of Jesus and who pointed to the Lamb of God who takes away the sin of the world, must be taken for what it is: a testimony which can awaken our interest and make us seek further. It does not provide actual evidence; it is merely a challenge.

"But the testimony I have is greater than that of John; for the works which the Father has granted me to accomplish, these very works which I am doing, bear me witness that the Father has sent me."

Here again we find ourselves in the situation that we have not ourselves *seen* the works Jesus did, as his contemporaries saw them. All we have is the *record* of these works. To be sure, that is a powerful testimony—but can we believe it?

The Records Bear Witness

In addition we have the record of his works down through history. Does this convince us? Some will answer no. In spite of nearly two thousand years of opportunity, Christianity has not been able to solve the world's problems. Often it has been used as a pretext by people who were seeking power or money or honor for themselves.

It has been used as a pious cover for all sorts of godlessness and folly. Many times people have testified that they have tried Christianity, and that it has not helped them.

On the other hand, many of us acknowledge that we have met people for whom Christianity, or more correctly the living Christ, is real and mighty. Quite possibly we ourselves have memories of an occasion in which Christ intervened and took charge of our lives. Many can testify that they have had such experiences, even though they were not able to make their relationship to Jesus permanent.

When we speak of the works of Jesus we are dealing with something intensely personal, so the distance between us and him is not nineteen hundred years. People through the centuries have done their best to hinder his work and to make it powerless. No matter what the cost, we know that we must do all in our power to silence them.

The Scriptures Bear Witness

The next witness Jesus names is Scripture. What does it mean that the Bible appears as a witness for Christ in our day? Isn't it that this remarkable book, brought into being by nearly a hundred writers over a period of more than a thousand years, yet constitutes a unity, a living whole? Those who immerse themselves in the book discover a wonderful candelabrum whose rays meet at one point: "You search the scriptures, because you think that in them you have eternal life; and it is they that bear witness to me."

The Bible is the book about him who was to come, who came, who is here, and who some day will come again. For centuries God used men who understood little and discerned less, yet step by step they moved toward the Light.

Those who pick the Bible apart into separate passages, whether to contradict it or to demonstrate strange prophecies, lose the light. They find what they are looking for and nothing else. In the book no one finds more than he seeks, until he is found by the one who seeks him.

The Father Bears Witness

This is what Jesus points to when he names the fourth and most wonderful witness of all: "And the Father who sent me has himself borne witness to me. His voice you have never heard, his form you have never seen; and you do not have his word abiding in you, for you do not believe him whom he has sent."

Isn't that exactly the conclusion toward which we have been moving? We have been going in a circle and are now about to return to our starting point: You cannot believe because you will not believe; and you will not believe because you cannot believe. Or to put it another way: You must love the truth before you can know the truth —but who can love what he does not know?

A Matter of Trust

Faith and love are actually one and the same; they stem from the same root. The name of the root is *trust,* and trust stems from *devotion.* Trust does not grow from proof, but from conviction. A child trusts his father, not because he has studied his father's life and analyzed his character and personality, but because devotion builds a bridge from heart to heart.

Thus it is with all love, including that between a man and a woman. Who would ever say to his beloved, "Show me trustworthy proof that you love me" or "Give me a document proving that I can depend on you!" Demands like that would kill love, destroy everything that it means. When heart is open to heart, proofs form a barrier. Even the most solid guarantee becomes a wall to shut out warmth.

Truth is based on conviction and does not require proof. It seeks for communion with someone else. Only he who himself has an open heart understands the speech of an open heart. It requires "truth in the inward being" to accept the testimony of him who says, *"I am the truth."*

When testimony comes to us today from a John the Baptist; from prophets and apostles and a hundred nameless writers of the Scriptures; from the millions of saints of the church, that the miracle of Christmas is really our salvation—then the testimony of all these witnesses is much more than a historical source to be investigated. Rather it is a question which I personally must face: Do I accept the testimony of God's messengers concerning God's great messenger?

Or do I decide that I will get along just fine by myself? To depend on oneself is also a mode of life. But it is the exact opposite of Christmas—it is anti-Christmas. "Glory to me in the highest, and on earth peace, as long as people conform to my wishes." What a Christmas gospel! Amen.

HAPPINESS FOR EVERYONE

Luke 2:10   CHRISTMAS EVE MESSAGE TO CHILDREN

*Lord Jesus, make us happy in the right way. Help us to
make others happy and to make you happy, so that your
angels may sing for joy because of us. Amen.*

If I were to ask you, "What is the happiest day
of the year?" I am sure you would say Christmas
Eve. "I am so glad each Christmas Eve," we sing,
and "So glad are we, so glad are we." In a short
time we will be leaving the church to go home,
and I know that today there will be no loitering
along the way! At home are the Christmas tree
and the Christmas lights; all our dear ones are
there, and everything else that belongs to this
festival evening.

We are happy because it is Christmas, and that
is the way it should be. Remember what the angel
said to the shepherds: "Behold, I bring you good

news of a great joy which will come to all the people." If these words are a bit difficult to understand, let me tell you what they mean: "Listen carefully, because I am going to tell you something that is going to make you very happy, and everyone else is going to be happy with you."

Making Sad People Happy

If everything were as it should be, what we sing in one of our songs would be true: "On Christmas Eve will all be glad." But is that really so? I wonder if there are not some people who are sad this Christmas Eve, who cannot join us in singing "Joy to the world!"

I am sure there are people like that, and we who *are* happy should think about those who are sad. What counts here on earth, not only on Christmas Eve but every evening and morning and all day long is not only to be happy yourself, but to help those who are not happy.

Who are these people? Perhaps someone is sick, and cannot celebrate Christmas with his dear ones. Perhaps someone has lost someone so dear that he has no one with whom he wants to celebrate Christmas.

Perhaps someone has no place where he *can* celebrate Christmas. In some places of the world people are not permitted to go to church or to

observe Christmas even in their homes, because
the rulers of their countries do not want anyone
to celebrate a festival for Jesus. Thousands of
families have fled from these countries to other
lands where they will have freedom to live as they
want and to celebrate Christmas as we do. Some
of these refugees, as we call them, are living in
poverty and misery; it certainly can't be easy for
them to be happy!

We could go on naming different kinds of people who do not find it easy to be happy and who
perhaps find it especially hard at Christmas when
they remember the good times they had in their
old homes. Perhaps, too, they think of people like
us who are so happy.

If we are glad in the way the angels meant, we
want always and above all to think about making
those around us happy, too.

Birthdays Are Happy Days

And that brings me to a very important question: Do you think *Jesus* is happy today? Christmas is *his* festival, *his* birthday. Birthdays are
happy days for all who have a part in their celebration, but happiest of all for the one whose
birthday it is.

I want to tell you about a boy who moved to a
new home. Sometimes it is fun to move and to

make new friends. But it wasn't so easy for this boy. The boys in the new neighborhood weren't very kind to him. They teased him because he was new and his speech was a bit different from theirs.

Then something happened. The boys heard that the new boy was going to have a birthday. Then they all wanted to be friends—for that one day. Why do you suppose that was? Of course, they wanted to be invited to the birthday party. Some of them were invited and had a wonderful time all afternoon. But, believe it or not, they were just as mean as ever the next day. I am sure you will agree that that was pretty bad. It was bad enough to be mean the whole year through, and worse to be sneaky-friendly that one day just to get in on the party!

That brings me to something very sad. Don't all of us behave at least a little like that toward Jesus? On Christmas Eve we sing about Jesus, we go to church, we even think a little about him. We go to his birthday party with its Christmas tree, gifts, and good food. But are we his friends the rest of the year?

Do we think about him, do we talk with him, do we try to be the way he wants us to be? If we are truthful, we will have to admit that none of us, young or old, has been so kind to Jesus this past year that we have no reason to be ashamed today as we celebrate his birthday.

In a special way this question concerns us parents, who have the responsibility of influencing our children. What place does Jesus have day by day in *my* home? Is there time for prayer and song? Is the way to God's house kept open so that my children will travel it? Most important, do we *live* according to his Word?

Making Jesus' Birthday Happy

Is Jesus happy today? Is he glad as he sees us sitting in church? I think we must answer that he is both happy and sad. He is glad because we have come here to be with him on this festive day, but he is sad because we are with him so seldom the rest of the year. Perhaps he is saddest of all because even now our hearts are not fully with him.

> Jesus, alas! how can it be
> So few bestow a thought on Thee,
> Or on the love, so wondrous great,
> That drew Thee down to our estate?
> (LH 179, stanza 4)

We might think that the boy I told you about would have pushed his guests away and said, "Go home and learn to be kind; then you may come back next year." But he didn't, and neither does Jesus.

Jesus knows that we are not as good as we should be; that is why he came down to earth. It was not because we are so kind and good that he simply had to make a trip down here to enjoy our company. It was because we are so scatter-brained and disobedient and contrary that we would not be able to get to heaven by ourselves. Somebody had to help us.

Jesus did not go around gathering up people to be his friends because they were kind and good. He sought out people who were *not* kind and good and were troubled about it. To them he said, "Come here and be with me, and I will make you God's children anyway. I will help you so that you will become really happy, then other people will be happy with you."

When is Jesus happy? He is happy when he can make us happy. Being really happy doesn't mean having fun one evening of the year and then it is all over. The great joy the angels sang about Christmas night is the joy we experience when we understand that God loves us *in spite of every-thing*.

He loves us when we are disgusted with ourselves and angry with everybody else; when we have lost courage and when we are tired; when it seems nothing is right; and when we come to the end of life with no one to help us. Jesus comes to us when we don't quite know how to be glad.

He knows how to be happy, and he promises that we shall be with him always and that he will make us happy.

When we say to Jesus—and we don't need to say it out loud, we can whisper it so only he can hear it: "Dear Jesus, be with me and do for me all the good that I cannot do for myself"—then we make Jesus happy. That is what he came here for, and he wants us to let him help us. That is the birthday gift he wants from us. Then he becomes our friend, not only on his birthday but every day of the year. Dear children and dear grownups, today we will make Jesus glad—or sad.

If we let Jesus make us happy in the right way, we make him and all the angels in heaven glad. And we become the kind of people who help make others happy.

" 'For behold, I bring you news of a great joy which will come to all the people; for to you is born this day in the city of David a Savior, who is Christ the Lord. And this will be a sign for you: you will find a babe wrapped in swaddling cloths and lying in a manger.' And suddenly there was with the angel a multitude of the heavenly host praising God. . . . " Yes, that is joy, and it is ours. Amen.

GOD GAVE HIS SON

Luke 2:1-14   CHRISTMAS DAY

Welcome to earth, Thou noble Guest,
Through whom the sinful world is blest!
Thou com'st to share our misery,
What can we render, Lord, to Thee!

Ah, dearest Jesus, Holy Child,
Make Thee a bed, soft undefiled,
Within my heart, that it may be
A quiet chamber kept for Thee. Amen.

(LH, 181, stanzas 8, 13)

A blessed Christmas, dear congregation, and a blessed Christmas everyone, far and near, who joins us in this festival worship.

We have encountered that greeting many times already, not only today but last night, on Christmas Eve. And probably several days before that as friends have greeted each other joyfully: "A blessed Christmas, a joyous Christmas!" We have read it on greeting cards and posters, in newspapers and Christmas annuals. "A blessed Christmas, a joyous Christmas"—the greeting covers us with a flood of good will and warmth.

The Genuine "I"

I wonder if all this is genuine. Isn't it a bit amusing that I, who am often both grouchy and disgruntled, am suddenly gripped by Christmas goodness and find myself broadcasting Christmas cheer to all the world? Is this the actual *I* or is it something put on, a sort of mask acquired for use at Christmas time?

It is possible that the very opposite is true. Perhaps what happens to us at Christmas is that the mask falls away, the walls crumble, at least for a while. May it not be that Christmas brings out in me the genuine I, leading me back to the fundamental, the true? May it not be that it is the gloom of my everyday life which is false?

But these imaginings are in vain. I will never understand which is the genuine I—my Christmas personality or my everyday personality. Let me turn my back on my own confusion and self-contradiction and look at him who is truly genuine, the Savior of the world who is born today. If he dwells in my heart, then *he* is my real I! Then all the everyday lies and all the festival deceptions disappear and only he remains. Then Christmas becomes a festival not for a day, but for eternity.

> To us is born a blessed child,
>   To us a Son is given,
> Born of a virgin undefiled,
>   He is our hope of heaven;
> Had not this Child to us been born,
>   We all had been in sin forlorn,
>   He is our sole salvation;
> All thanks, Lord Jesus Christ, to Thee,
>   That Thou wert pleased a man to be:
>   Save us from condemnation!
>
> (LH 189)

"Christmas" Means "Give"

"Christmas" is a simple and familiar word, but how much it includes: memories, longing, happiness. Among the treasures it contains is an even simpler word which tells better than any other what Christmas really is—the word "give." Let us not think first of the gifts under the tree or of our depleted pocketbooks. Although the custom of giving gifts at Christmas does get out of hand at times, it is a lovely custom.

"Give." This little word sends its rays of light in three directions: there is first a *giver*, secondly a *gift*, and thirdly one who *receives*. As we enter Christmas, we must pause at all three.

The Giver

Christmas means a gift from God. "Every good endowment and every perfect gift is from above, coming down from the Father of lights with whom there is no variation or shadow due to change," says Scripture.

Many protest that they have sought God but have found nothing. "For me 'God' is only a word. I do not know him, and no one has been able to point him out for me."

The wise men of the world reason that God is hidden and that no one can know anything about him. They are right; the Bible itself emphasizes that. "No one has ever seen God," says the evangelist. The apostle says of him that he "dwells in unapproachable light, whom no man has ever seen or can see." But the evangelist also says, "The only Son, who is in the bosom of the Father, he has made him known."

That is the heart of the matter. Even though the giver dwells in a land closed to us, we can know him because he has sent us his gift. "For God so loved the world that he gave his only Son, that whoever believes in him should not perish but have eternal life." That gift tells us about the giver, for Jesus said, "He who has seen me has seen the Father."

The Gift

Next we look at the gift. The little child in the manger is the greatest treasure ever given on earth. In him God has come to us. Our attempts to find him led nowhere, nor did our efforts to flee from him. Our good will was not strong

enough to lift us up to the light, nor was our
evil will so strong that we were satisfied with the
darkness.

So the gift comes to us, bewildered and perverse
as we are. It is God himself who comes to us who
have cast aside God's kingdom and attempted to
form one of our own. He does not come in daz-
zling majesty, or with glory which would cripple
sense and sight, or in a flame which would destroy
us. He comes as the most gentle and unobtrusive
one among us.

God in a stable and a manger. God the almighty
and the all-knowing revealed in the innocence of
a tiny infant. God, to whom the universe belongs,
born in rags and poverty. Can't you imagine the
headlines if it happened today: "Welfare Scandal
in Judea," "Child Born in a Stable," "No Room
for a Child."

Is this, then, the Christian picture of the Lord
of the universe? Yes. The church does not proclaim a God who dwells millions of light-years beyond our solar system, shaking his head dubious-
ly. Nor does the church permit God to become a
synonym for nature. God is living, personal—a
Father who wishes us well. This he proved by
entering our lives and sharing our circumstances,
and he did it completely, entirely, without limita-
tion. His is the manger and the cross.

Look at his hands — the hands of the infant

reaching out to grasp the sun's rays, the hands of
the sufferer stretched out along the arms of the
cross. Can we not see that these are *our* hands?
Even today, when they grasp the scepter of the
Almighty, they are our hands. He made himself
one with the weakest and the most miserable, so
that none might be forgotten before God. He
came to us all, and now no one needs to feel lost.

The prophets gave us a wonderful name to call
him: "Immanuel." It means "God is with us."
We may not be able to find God nor to understand him. But we have been given a manger to
kneel by. God has made himself helpless so that
we may be sure he came to help the helpless. "For
thus says the high and lofty One who inhabits
eternity, whose name is Holy: 'I dwell in the high
and holy place, and also with him who is of a contrite and humble spirit, to revive the spirit of the
humble, and to revive the heart of the contrite' "
(Isaiah 57:15).

This is the gift offered to all of us who know
our own poverty, who see our own weakness. Can
you imagine anything greater than that God himself, the eternal source of goodness, reaches out to
me—that he is with me and I with him, one in
time and in eternity? There is nothing so difficult
but that he enters into it and frees me from it.
There is nothing so glorious but that he pours it
into my hands.

Christmas means to give. We have seen the giver: the invisible God who becomes visible because he gives. We have seen the gift: a child in a manger, heaven in everyday dress.

The One Who Receives

Now, who is the third person in the picture, the one who receives? "Behold, I bring you good news of a great joy which will come to all the people." The address on the gift is plain enough. No one can say that he has been forgotten. The gift is intended for all. Therefore no one can accept it without at once passing it on, to his neighbor across the way, to his neighbor in Nigeria or New Guinea.

However, to be an addressee and to be a recipient are not the same thing. It doesn't help to receive all the letters in the world if I don't open them. "He came to his own home, and his own people received him not." There both the joy and sadness of Christmas are expressed. One thing is necessary: I must accept the gift. It is not mine until I let it become mine.

Can I say yes to the Christmas giver today? I cannot go to Bethlehem and enter the stable as the shepherds and the wise men did. But wait— perhaps I can. "And this will be a sign for you." These words echo through the world today, too.

His church is the stable, and there the manger stands. The church with its faults and failings, its sins and weaknesses—here are the hay and the straw where he may be found. The baptismal water which he consecrates, the bread and the wine, the book which brings his message, the humble people who gather for worship—all this is Bethlehem. These are the surroundings in which the Master meets us today.

One thing more: "Truly I say to you, as you did it to one of the least of these my brethren, you did it to me." The child in the humble manger, planted among an oppressed people, says to us, "Go with your gold, your frankincense and myrrh, to your brothers and sisters who are waiting. Even as I became your brother, so are they your brothers; it is I who await you in them." The Lord of lords does not dwell far away; he lives among the people of the world, he is one of us.

Can we not see all this, we who gather together with all the generations of two thousand years, we who hear the heavenly words and experience the holy and changeless sacraments? He dwells with us today. The manger has been planted here on earth.

Here is the giver, here is the gift. Where is the one to receive the gift? God's hands are filled to overflowing, eager to give. God is celebrating Christmas. Amen.

CHRISTMAS IN OUR SORT OF WORLD

Matthew 23:34-39   ST. STEPHEN'S DAY

Lord, may we never be poor in the peace of Christmas, and may we never be weak in the warfare of Christmas. "Let us in the midst of strife taste the peace you send us." Amen.

Since early times December 26 has been observed as St. Stephen's Day. It is also, of course, the Second Day of Christmas, and it is not too easy to combine the two. What possible connection can there be between the first Christmas and the first martyr? The ancient church put it this way: "Yesterday Christ was born on earth, so that today Stephen can be born in heaven." In the midst of the hatred and threatenings of the world, he gained the peace of Christmas and "entered Paradise with a song."

65

December 26 was assigned to Stephen and designated as the Festival of Martyrs long before it seemed necessary to assign a day for the celebration of the birthday of Jesus. December 25 became the birthday of Jesus simply because it seemed fitting to choose the day of the great Roman Festival of the Sun. Christ is the true sun, so it seemed logical to celebrate his birth on the day of "the unconquered sun."

Humanly speaking, therefore, it is coincidence which has placed Christmas and Stephen together. But I wonder if it was not God who placed good Stephen in the midst of the Christmas festival. Stephen seems incongruous from the purely secular view of Christmas, but for the conscience which is not entirely asleep, he becomes an admonishing reminder.

What Stephen Stands For

Stephen stands as a living witness to the fact that "Christmas" is not a synonym for "idyll." The peace of Christmas is not the same as freedom from strife; the joy of Christmas is not the same as freedom from sorrow; our meeting with the new life in the manger is not the same as freedom from death.

This old world whirls on in the same old way; indeed, it seems to become worse and worse. To all the old sins a new sin, the greatest of all, is added: the light shone in the darkness, but the darkness would not receive it. For the one who does accept Christ a new pain is added, the pain of seeing his hope rejected and his witness spurned, and of seeing himself cast out because of this very hope and witness.

Stephen stands here today to remind us of all this. He makes things uncomfortable for everyone who basks peacefully in a sort of blessed and comforting Christmas emotion. He stands here as a challenge and a question we cannot escape. The Christmas we have just celebrated and the happiness we have enjoyed—are these the actual Christmas? Stephen asks the question, and we must answer.

Our sermon text is a portion of Jesus' lament over Jerusalem, the city that made it a practice to kill the prophets who were sent to it and which finally nailed Christ to the cross. But Jerusalem is no better or worse than any other city. If the capital of our country does not equal Jerusalem's record for persecuting prophets, the only reason is probably that our city has not been blessed with an overwhelming number of prophets. Here, too, preachers and other witnesses to the truth have been spurned; it happens every day. Of course we do not use stones, but contempt and scorn are often just as effective in killing a man.

Can we make the whole thing simple by main-
taining that the truth has always been persecuted
here on earth? Isn't it true that most people prefer falsehood to truth, and for that reason witnesses to the truth are spurned while those who
serve falsehood are honored?

If it were as easy as that, it would be quite
simple to be a human being. We who by nature
love to irritate people and are disposed to be
quarrelsome would then be considerably closer
to the truth than others. Furthermore, we would
then stand the best chance of making the necessary
number of enemies here on earth so that we would
be assured of having a sufficient number of jewels
for our eternal crown!

No, it is not that simple. A Christian has a
heartfelt longing for peace, friendship and understanding with all his fellow men. A Christian is
every man's friend; he who is every man's friend
is a Christian. That statement is just as true and
just as false as if we said: A Christian is every
man's enemy; he who is every man's enemy is a
Christian. The Christian is in exactly the same
situation as his Master. Was Jesus every man's
enemy, or was he every man's friend?

We cannot answer that question by a simple
yes or no, because Jesus was both at the same
time. "He came to his own home, and his own
people received him not." He was like the friend

who stops a person intent on committing suicide. It is likely that the friend finds himself involved in a violent fight with the would-be suicide, who does not *want* to be saved.

A genuine Christian will probably always encounter feelings of opposition from those around him. His efforts to be honest, helpful, and understanding may win respect, but at the same time there is something about him which awakens fear and repugnance.

Running Away from God

Perhaps the simplest explanation is that we human beings are running away from God; we are afraid of having an actual encounter with him. A voice deep inside us asks, "Is it possible that God is right and I am wrong?" We try to throttle that voice and forget it, to think of something else. And if we are going to succeed in thinking about something else, it is essential that those we associate with shall also be thinking of something else.

In this way, without any specific agreement about it, all those who are fleeing from God form a sort of defensive alliance: If you will help me to escape, I will help you. If there are enough of us, we will succeed! We establish our own type of association with each other and tacitly agree on what subjects we will talk about. And so we help each other keep God safely out of our thoughts.

When one of us breaks this defensive alliance, the rest of us feel that that person is a traitor. When one of us is converted and testifies concerning the new life he has found, he causes offense and becomes painfully conspicuous. It goes against tact and good fellowship to talk that way, at our jobs, in the family circle, or wherever it may be. One just doesn't do that!

Such witness by word and action embarrasses us. It is an annoying reminder of what we want to forget more than anything else. It makes it difficult for us to rest comfortably in the peace we imagine that we, and most of the congenial folks we associate with, have arrived at.

So the Christian becomes an enemy, a disturber of the peace. A person who causes annoyance wherever he goes will soon feel the punishment of the world whose tranquility he has disturbed. And often that punishment is severe.

How does all this harmonize with the Christmas message of the peace and joy which shall be to all the people? It doesn't! It is exactly the same situation found in the words, "He came to his own people, and his own people received him not."

In a way we could say that this was the Master's own fault. Surely he could have slanted his message a bit so as to meet the desires of all those people! Then the result would have been, "He came to his own people, and his own people received him with open arms."

But wait! In that case *they* would not have been *his, he* would have been *theirs.* He could not make himself their servant and help them to flee still farther from God. He was the servant of the Lord and he had come to stop them in their flight, to open a way back for them to the Paradise they had forsaken. So they were filled with hatred toward the one who would close the way they had chosen. Thus it came about that the Lord's servant became the suffering servant, "despised and rejected by men; a man of sorrows and acquainted with grief."

The joy of Christmas is for everyone; it is given generously to all who kneel at the manger and accept it. But that does not mean that it is a mild and comforting emotion to be used by people who are fleeing from God. The tinsel and glitter, the stars, the children around a Christmas tree warm the heart and make it easy for us to imagine that all is well. If we feel ourselves sufficiently moved, we think that our Lord must be equally moved and will conclude that we are not so bad after all.

There is judgment in today's text. But Jesus speaks of judgment to show us the judgment that hangs over our lives, in order that we may escape it while there is still time. This we can do not by closing our eyes, not by seeking the help of neighbors and friends, not by attempting to forget it in a sort of Christmas-joy feeling. We escape judgment by accepting its justice, by acknowledging our real condition, and by learning to reach out toward the new hope which was lighted Christmas night.

In other words, we *accept salvation,* and that is possible for even the most hardened. Jesus closes his words of judgment over Jerusalem with these words: "You will not see me again, until you say, 'Blessed be he that comes in the name of the Lord.' "

May we be blessed in all eternity! Amen.

HEAVEN'S MELODY IS NOT SILENCED

Luke 1:68-75   SUNDAY AFTER CHRISTMAS

Lord, let the song of Christmas echo not only on our lips but also in the hearts of all who today hear thy Word, especially those who feel that they are outside the Christmas circle. Amen.

Today's text should not have been read; it should have been sung. This song of praise has been heard in the Christian church down through the ages. It is "Zechariah's Song of Praise," or, more simply "Benedictus"—"Blessed." "Blessed be the Lord God of Israel, for he has visited and redeemed his people."

This is a fitting day for today, for Christmas is the season of song. We join hands around the Christmas tree and let the melodies of Christmas resound. Even the most unmusical among us find ourselves singing this one day of the year. There is an old saying that "song unites," and surely the melodies of Christmas form a bond which unites heart with heart. The circle around our Christmas tree becomes a symbol of the greater circle of all who take part in the great song of praise which is Christmas.

> From east to west, from shore to shore,
> Let every heart awake and sing
> The holy Child whom Mary bore,
> The Christ, the everlasting King.
> (SBH 20, stanza 1)

The Melody Unites

Can't we see the host of those who join us as we gather to praise the royal child in the manger? They come from every race, from every part of the earth, from every Christian Church. Catholics and Protestants, Lutherans and Pentecostals—what separates them seems insignificant compared with what unites them: the Christ child born among us. Even among those who do not know him are some who are seeking the truth, and through some means which only God knows, we can hope they reach the same goal. He who is born into the world came to embrace us all; let us therefore do all we can to see that the Gospel of joy reaches them all!

The Bethlehem pilgrimage is a never-ending procession. It includes not only this generation, but reaches back into our fathers and our fathers'

fathers. We join hands with all the generations who have found the way to the stable and the manger since that first Christmas night.

"From east to west, from shore to shore" is a hymn from the early church. "Triumph ye heavens" comes from the eighteenth century. The nineteenth century gave us "I am so glad each Christmas Eve." From the Middle Ages came "A Child is born in Bethlehem," and "Good Christian men rejoice, with heart and soul and voice." And the ancient church sang, "All glory be to God on high, who hath our race befriended." From the dawning of Christianity to the present, the worship of the church has included songs of glory to God in the highest and peace on earth.

So vast is the chain that unites us that the hymn writer did not go far enough when he said that the "angels from the realms of glory" sang first for the shepherds. The angels were the first to testify, "It has come to pass." But long before that there were voices who rejoiced because it was to happen. The long procession of those singing Christmas praises began before Christmas came, and the singers of expectation belong here fully as much as the singers of fulfillment.

The Promise to Zechariah

Zechariah was one of those who waited. Although he had not yet seen what was to happen,

he had a promise from God to cling to. His joy
was just as real as the joy of the shepherds and the
wise men a few months later. Zechariah belongs
in the Christmas circle, and he knows exactly why
he is there. That makes him an ideal song leader
for us as we join hands around the Christmas tree.
Do we see as clearly as he that God wants to do
something for us at Christmas, and what he wants
to do?

Zechariah knows, not because he has figured it
out himself, but because God told him, not only
directly but through his messengers for centuries
past. Zechariah includes everyone in his message
from God, saying that God has sent us salvation
"as he spoke by the mouth of his holy prophets of
old." So the prophets belong in the circle too,
those courageous advance guards of expectation.

The manger at Bethlehem is history's center,
and around it gather all generations, past and future. Isaiah belongs there, and Micah, and Zechariah—more accurately *two* Zechariahs, the prophet of the Old Testament by that name and our
Zechariah, the father of John the Baptist. These
prophets planted the seed of expectation in a
chosen people, a people chosen in order that they
might some day bring the fulfillment to all the
world.

We owe so much to waiting Israel, and how
poorly Christianity has rewarded this people. How

quick we have been to turn them away from the circle to which they should as a matter of course belong!

Here there are no boundaries of nations or peoples or time. All those who have received from God the "good news of a great joy" and who have voiced it in song—melodiously or not—have a place in the Christmas circle.

Our Father Abraham

Doesn't the procession have a beginning? Our text names Abraham, father of the chosen people. God's work of salvation began, in a sense, the day Abraham journeyed out into an uncertain future with nothing to rely upon but God's promise, "By you all the families of the earth will bless themselves." There is little concerning Abraham that historians can say with certainty, but that creates no difficulty for our faith. The picture which Genesis draws for us is a testimony to the light which the great men of God found and by which they and their followers lived and died.

Yet, can we say that it was really with Abraham's venture of faith that it all began? The Bible pictures an earlier Noah, an Enoch, an Abel. Doesn't the promise shine over the very first guilt-laden human beings? The seed of the woman was to crush the serpent's head, Scripture says. This means that as long as there have been human beings, they have lived under the star of hope. God's promises have been given to the entire human race.

The circle which meets at Christ's manger is endless. Toward it point every loss, every longing, every question, every anxiety and every regret. From it shine all joy, all strength, all courage, and all the future. Everyone belongs here.

> Come then, let us hasten yonder;
>   Here let all, great and small,
> Kneel in awe and wonder,
> Love him who with love is yearning;
>   Hail the star that from far
> Bright with hope is burning.
>
> (SBH 26, stanza 3)

"Blessed be the Lord God of Israel, for he has visited and redeemed his people, and has raised up a horn of salvation for us in the house of his servant David, as he spake by the mouth of his holy prophets from of old."

"A horn of salvation"—what is that? In all likelihood the expression refers to one of the ancient laws of Israel. The altar in the Holy Place of the Temple had horns, which were probably small pillars, rising from each corner of the altar. A miserable wretch, guilty or innocent, who was being pursued could gain sanctuary by hurrying to the altar and grasping one of those horns. As long as he remained there he shared in the sacred power of the altar and no one dared touch him.

Safe From Our Enemies

The meaning is clear. The Bethlehem manger is our place of refuge This is the point of Zechariah's Christmas song: "that we should be saved from our enemies." God has promised his people freedom from the power of their enemies.

Doesn't it seem incongruous to mingle enmity with the joy of the Christmas festival? No, the enemy has a place here. The great strife we have been thrown into knows no pause, not even on a holy Christmas Eve, much less on an ordinary Sunday.

If there were no enemy, we would have no need of a Christmas Gospel. The real enemy is not named Augustus or Herod, nor even Mao. If we remain alert we can protect ourselves from such enemies. It is much harder to deal with the enemy which is within ourselves. If we looked into our own hearts with the same eagerness we often look into the lives of our neighbors, the chances are pretty good that we would discover that enemy!

I am the enemy. I know very little about the power which makes me worship the mighty *I*. But it is there, and I have a distinct feeling that around me whirl invisible beings which sing their own

Christmas song: "Glory to me in the highest, and peace on earth as long as people let me have my own way!"

When a person robs God in the way I have done, the result is inevitable. The idol named "I" steals away my power, and I am filled with the demons of envy, suspicion, pride and hypocrisy. Weak as I am, I cannot chase them away nor silence their voices.

It is from such a tyranny that I am promised release. The King's son came down to earth, sings Zechariah, "that we, being delivered from the hand of our enemies, might serve him (God) without fear, in holiness and righteousness before him all the days of our life."

That, good Christian friends, is the melody of Christmas. All who reach out for this salvation are on the way to the manger and belong in the Christmas circle. But let us not forget that it is possible to go around the Christmas tree with one's back to Bethlehem. And, sadly, it is also possible for the melody of Christmas to fill our mouths while our hearts remain empty. Amen.

IN YOUR HAND

Psalm 31:14-16   NEW YEAR'S EVE

Help us, O God, to look honestly at our days and at the Lord of our days, so that we may understand them and know you. Amen.

Some years ago one of our boys, who was about four at the time, asked a very philosophical question: "Mother, where are the days that haven't come yet?" I can't recall what the answer was, but it is doubtful that it could compare in profundity with the question. What sort of answer can we give to such a question?

Of course we can try to convince the child that his question is based on a misunderstanding, that the days are not anywhere. A philosopher would answer that time simply cannot be brought into the room with us in visible form. We can stand beside a highway and ask "Where are the cars

that haven't passed yet?" They are somewhere—
here, there, somewhere else—and if I cannot see
them, someone else can. It is even possible to stop
the cars whizzing by; their continued progress is
not inevitable.

But our little boy was mistaken when he imag-
ined that the days roll by like a column of cars.
The days that have not come yet simply do not
exist. No man can see them, no one can stop them.
They are outside man's reach.

Not only the days, but the hours, minutes, and
seconds are out of our reach. The next second cannot be found, nor can the second that just passed.
The same would be true if a second were divided
into ten parts, even into a thousand parts. There
is never a "now," because time never stands still,
it can never be grasped and held. Time flows past
like a stream which no one can stop. Along the
highway of time are no traffic barriers.

The days which have not come simply do not
exist, and it does no good to attempt to find them.
Even today has no existence. In part it is lost in
the great nothingness of the past, in part it is
hidden in the great uncertainty of the future. We
stand on the invisible line where future becomes
past without any "by your leave" from us. Time
is something that happens around us, with us, in
us, and never can we do anything about it. Time
is fate—deaf and dumb and inexorable.

The Dwelling Place of Time

True as this is, when it has been said we feel that something important is lacking. Time does have a dwelling place—in our minds. The days *live* there, they *are* there, they *rule* there. The days that are gone live in harmony. The days that are to come live in anticipation. Their existence within me is just as real and decisive as the experience of a place on the map.

The days that are gone—there is surely something to say about them. There are days that I wish I could call back, happy days that I wish could have lasted forever. But I cannot call them back. Memory gives me some comfort, but I realize sadly that it is a poor substitute for life itself. The more often I recall those days, the more worn they become. Their original colors become more faded every time I remember, until at last I do not know what is the original fact and what has been added through the constant process of recall. Memories become worn by being called back, but memories that are not recalled also wear out.

Then there are the days which we would like to forget but from which we cannot free ourselves. There are memories of stupidity, weakness, sins; memories of sorrows and blows which fate has dealt us. The evil days creep out again and again when I am not on my guard, and try as I will to show them the door, they hang on tight!

Memories, in short, are evidence that I am not master of my past. The days I want to hold get away from me, and I cannot escape the days that want to hold me. The past owns me, but I cannot make myself its master.

It is the same with the days that lie ahead. They live their remarkable lives *in* me and have their unchangeable ways *with* me. I cannot avoid them. The future exists in my anticipation of it, in my happy expectations, my plans, my dreams, in what I hope will come to be. Hope is the boundary between dream and reality. Without any decision on my part, I suddenly find myself thrust into the future.

It is true also of my forebodings concerning the future, both those I build out of my own experience, and those based on the condition of the world and on newspaper headlines. The bright dreams and the dark forebodings of the future are a different mixture for different people, depending on temperament and disposition, and to some extent on age and circumstances and even which newspapers one reads!

Both the beautiful fantasies and the forebodings of evil are actually expressions of my powerlessness and my utter dependence on a future which I may be able to influence to a very small extent and which ultimately is determined by forces which are *not* mine.

I look about me here on earth,
I think of days gone by,
Of those that went and those that came,
And what is yet to be.

The conclusion is inevitable: I am the victim of a constantly shifting stream of events. The best I can do by my own efforts is to change ever so slightly my position in the stream. There is no possibility of escape from the stream; that stream has no bank to offer me escape. Wherever I try to steer my life, my eyes meet only the overpowering waters of the future.

These fleeting hours and days and years of mine, can they not be found in some place other than my mind? Isn't it possible some way to hold them so that I can escape this continuing captivity in the whirling streams of fate?

God's Hand or Ours?

The text for this closing hour of the year gives the answer: "My times are in thy hand." If we could only make that vision ours! In God's hand many, many things become different.

Is it possible that our tragedy lies in the perversion we make of that verse from the psalm? We say, "My times are in *my* hand." I build my own happiness. How this self-esteem seems to be a part of everyone! We meet it even in little children. "I want to hold it myself! Let me do it myself!" If Father takes a spoonful of food to give the child, the child insists on putting it back on the plate so that he can feed himself. "Do it myself! Do it myself!"

It is true that under many circumstances this will to do it oneself is valuable. But as a total program of life it will not suffice because it can live and grow only in the soil of illusion, the illusion that I hold tomorrow in my hand and that my plans and calculations will succeed. Then when trials set in and the world develops differently from the way I thought it would, I have nowhere to turn. Transition, change, death—these are the forces which ruin my plans.

The crossroads of life forces me to think more seriously of these things and remind me painfully that my hands are not strong enough or steady enough to bear so great a load. New Year's Eve, with its reminder that another year is ending, should be such a crossroad. It makes everything shake under me; it unveils all my illusions. Some day these hands of mine will sink to earth, final proof that my reckoning has been false.

In this world of ours where we all play with the idea of being self-sufficient, there was one who in the last moments of his life cried out, "Father, into thy hands I commit my spirit!" He possessed something which sustained him, even in the last dark nightwatch: "Into thy hands."

It is God's hand which reaches out to us through the Word which we are hearing today. It is God's hand which offers to guard us. It is the hand which guides the course of the world even when we cannot see it, and which never lets go of even the smallest in times of need and danger. "Humble yourself therefore under the mighty hand of God, that in due time he may exalt you. Cast all your anxieties on him, for he cares for you." So speaks the apostle.

Past, Present and Future Belong to God

My times are in the hand of the Almighty, the times that are behind me and those that are before me. All that was bright and good and glorious is not gone. It is preserved for all eternity; it is in God's hand. Much which I did not understand will be explained. I will understand that in God's hand even the seemingly bitter and meaningless has been given meaning. In the world of faith, there is nothing that does or does not have meaning. Meaning is something that is created wherever God's mighty hand is permitted to use our experiences as tools to mold the human heart.

In that hand, too, are my sins—but not to be kept there. Many have been able to exult with old King Hezekiah: "Lo, it was for my welfare that I had great bitterness; but thou hast held back my life from the pit of destruction, for thou hast cast all my sins behind thy back" (Isaiah 38:17). God's hand is able not only to hold fast but also to let go.

The future, the uncertain future, also rests in the same hand. In that knowledge we are secure. "For I am sure that neither death, nor life, nor angels, nor principalities, nor things present, nor things to come, nor powers, nor height, nor depth, nor anything else in all creation, will be able to separate us from the love of God in Christ Jesus our Lord." There is nothing more to say.

The fact that the future rests in God's hand does not mean that it will necessarily seem sweet and pleasant as it passes by. But it does mean that nothing can happen which will not be a blessing to the one who *permits* himself to be blessed, who humbles himself under the mighty hand of God, and casts all his sorrows where loving care is to be found. This is true even of what seems meaningless. "You meant evil against me," said Joseph to his brothers, "but God meant it for good to bring it about that many people should be kept alive."

So where are they, the days which have not yet come? Where are they, the 365 days which will make up the year which now begins? They are in our plans. They are in our hopes. They are in our anxieties. We try to grasp them and hold them fast, only to discover that we lay hold of shadows.

When it comes down to it, our days are in one place only: "My times are in thy hand."

Let them remain there. And let us place ourselves and our days in those hands. There is room for them, and there is room for us. Amen.

FRUIT

Our Lord and Master, who looks into our innermost beings in this new year as in the old, we pray that you would pluck out of us as many false views of life as we can get along without, so that the truth may do its work in our hearts. Amen.

It seems too bad that the unfruitful fig tree is not given an opportunity to speak, that it is condemned to listen in complete silence to the conversation between the master and his gardener. After all, the tree has a vital concern in this affair, and we imagine that it would have a few things to say. I can hear the fig tree reasoning like this:

"My dear master, of course I can understand your impatience because I have not borne fruit. At the same time I object emphatically to your statement that I have used up the ground to no avail. That is simply not true. My beautiful green leaves have caught the sunlight and have shared with all the other green trees and plants the work of creating organic nourishment by combining elements of the air with elements of the ground. And isn't that necessary if life is to be preserved on earth? Furthermore, my beauty has given happiness to many eyes. My blossoms are as beautiful as any in the garden. In my branches the birds have sung and the wind has whispered of spring and warmth. On the grounds of these undeniable facts, I maintain that I have not lived in vain, that I have not used up the ground to no avail."

Even if the fig tree could have spoken, its words probably would not have made much of an impression on the owner of the vineyard. He would probably have answered something like this:

"Even if we agree that everything you say is true, I will have to stand by what I said. It was I who assigned you a place in my garden. It was I who permitted the gardener to put a fence around you and take care of you. I did all this because I had a purpose in mind for you. I expected something specific from you. I expected fruit. What you say does not alter the fact that *I have received no fruit.* You have not fulfilled your purpose. The ground you have occupied was intended for a tree that would bear figs."

I ask you to imagine this conversation to emphasize one thing. It may be difficult for many of

us to recognize ourselves in the role of the unfruitful fig tree. Our year-end reckonings show that
we really have accomplished this and that in the
year that is just ended. Some of us are more satisfied than others, to be sure, and probably none of
us attained quite everything we had hoped for.
But can't we agree that we left behind us at least
a few footprints? By and large we have been useful citizens who have done our duty decently. If
anyone accuses us of having occupied the ground
to no avail, surely we have a right to enter an em-
phatic objection.

What Does God Expect of Us?

With all our protests, however, we have not
answered the penetrating question of our text.
Even if the leaves and the blossoms, the roots and
the branches have functioned irreproachably, the
question remains: *What of the fruit?* Before we
can answer that we must answer a related question: What fruit does God expect of me?

The shortest and simplest answer is this: The
fruit God expects is a thankful heart. He expects
me to be guided by a thankful heart—and that
wherever I go other hearts will be filled with
thanksgiving.

How many hearts did I fill with gratitude last
year? Isn't that the most accurate scale on which

to weigh the fruit I bore? A thankful heart is a costly fruit which gleams with beauty in God's sight.

To live our human lives as God has intended that we should involves a great deal more than, and something entirely different from, living correctly and as good citizens. To live is to awaken to an ever new and greater wonder at God's goodness, and to pour out that wonder to all the world. To live is to picture God in such a way that he begins to live in the consciousness of those who know you. That is what it means to bear fruit.

When this has been said we feel a little embarrassed for the unfruitful fig tree which tried so hard to excuse itself by prattling about its lovely leaves. If it is possible for a person to bear fruit for God by spreading seed which contains the promise of future life, then everything else becomes secondary. It is more blessed to be a small, crippled bush which bears one single fig than to be the largest, most beautiful tree in the garden which has nothing to boast of but blossoms and leaves and height.

It does no good to argue with the master of the vineyard. He is not satisfied with something just because it glitters in our eyes. He asks just one thing: Has his purpose in us been attained? Has that purpose reached those he wanted to reach? Has the great joy of Paradise resulted in fruit which has made my life meaningful for my fellow men?

We stand face to face with a new year. Quite possibly many of you said to yourselves when the text was read: "Was it really necessary for him to begin the year with a scolding? Wouldn't it be better if we received encouragement and something to strengthen us, rather than these warnings of disaster about inspection, the axe, a speedy trial and condemnation for the tree which has not come up to expectations?"

I wonder if such a question does not reveal a misunderstanding. Today's text does not have the purpose of scolding us. Its message is not "Look out! If you do not mend your ways, this will be your last New Year's Day." To be sure, it is quite possible that last year was the final year for some of us. That no one knows, and it is a possibility that we are not able to hide from.

But that gives us no right to falsify the text. The parable of the unfruitful fig tree does not contain a single admonition. Nobody shouts "boo" at the tree; nobody issues the command, "Pull yourself together." Nothing is said about anything the tree must do—only what the gardener has done and intends to do in order that the tree may have another chance. Everything is to be done to make it possible for the tree to fulfill its purpose. The tree is not to be uprooted as long as there is the slightest possibility that it may be helped. For the tree there is hope.

Joy and Hope for the New Year

So it is the *Gospel,* tidings of great joy, that greets us on this first day of the year. Rejoice! God has done for you the greatest of the great; he has planted you as a tree in his garden. He has done everything to make it possible for you to bear fruit which endures. In the days that lie ahead, he will spare nothing to help you reach the goal.

It is enough to make one faint with joy. Christianity not only affirms that God puts up with me in spite of my evil deeds and forgives even my most notorious sins. Christianity is more than that: God takes me into his service, he finds joy in my imperfect efforts, he blesses my fellow men through my feeble goodness. He makes use of what I do and makes it his own. We are God's arms in the world. We are the branches which bear his most precious fruit.

When we look at our own dubious motives and see how, even in our finest hours, we pose and try to make ourselves something special in the eyes of others—then it seems fantastic that God can and does acknowledge any part of our lives as his. But that is the way it is. The Bible says it, and the history of Christianity testifies to it. *God uses people.*

Where I see only empty stalks and stunted fruit on my own branches, God sees ripe fruit. Even my fellow men see it that way, so that I feel embarrassed and ashamed when it dawns on me how the master of the vineyard has rejoiced over the least successful tree in the garden. What a wonderful God! "By this my Father is glorified that you bear much fruit, and so prove to be my disciples. . . . You did not choose me, but I chose you and appointed you that you should go and bear fruit and that your fruit should abide; so that whatever you ask the Father in my name, he may give it to you."

Jesus spoke these words, and it is easy to recognize him in the gardener who interceded so warmly for the tree. Of course there is nothing in the parable itself which compels us to seek the identity of the master and the gardener. It is clear that the master is God, but his conversation could either be a figurative description of God taking counsel with himself or a conference with his Son.

The Meaning of Calvary

Nevertheless it is fitting to connect the gardener with Jesus. The self-sacrificing effort to save the condemned tree reached its climax in

Christ's sacrifice on Calvary. There love gave the most, there love won the most. There the fruit of eternity once and for all ripened on the tree of life. The tree of the cross is the tree whose branches bear fruit beyond all the fruits of the earth. Even its roots send out shoots which become new trees, and from its sprouts can grow fruit which lasts eternally.

That is why we begin our new year in Jesus' name. We place ourselves, with all the days that are past and all that lie ahead, in his hand. We say to him, "I can count on you; you will never give me up. You have forgiveness for my past and promises for my future. No matter what happens, I can count on you. You who have planted my roots in the earth of God's kingdom will do everything to make the new year for me all that God intends, and to make *me* be for *God* all that he wants."

This year, success and good fortune may ripen the figs. But it may also be that struggles and difficult times will teach me to bear fruit in patience. That is the most precious fruit of all, because it makes it possible for us to feel with our fellow men and to enter into their lives and bring them God's peace in their trials. "Blessed be the God and Father of our Lord Jesus Christ, the Father of mercies and God of all comfort, who comforts us in all our affliction, so that we may be able to comfort those who are in any affliction, with the comfort with which we ourselves are comforted by God."

> You cleanse my heart with tend'rest hand;
> Though bleeds the branch, it yet bears fruit.

If the new year brings me one step closer to my neighbor so that his sorrows and joys become my sorrows and joys, and my joy and peace become his, then this year will not have been lived in vain. Not for me, and not for those whose paths cross mine.

It has been said that God never lets us see the fruits we bear because we would eat them ourselves. It is true that nothing is more dangerous than to enjoy one's own good deeds. What counts is not *I* and *my* fruits, but the God and the neighbor for whom the fruit is intended. Do not count your good works, rather count the number of people who can use them! When you most completely forget yourself, your own spiritual growth, and your most beautiful fruit because you have so much to do for those who seek your help, then our Lord's harvest is richest.

We look to the future with confidence and with the assurance of growth in good days and evil, with the promise that the love of Christ will transform both the joyful and the sorrowful so that everything helps make the tree a genuine fruit-bearing tree in the great garden of the world.

Whatever happens or does not happen, I am safe from the tragedy of tragedies—that someday the words will be pronounced over my life: "Of no account!" What the great Lord of the vineyard puts his hand to is never lost. But before eternity begins, the tree which is my life must bear fruit to the glory of God. Amen.

MANY STARS - AND ONE STAR

Matthew 2:1-12

Dear Lord, there are so many people, so many races, so many nations. May the star you have lighted reach them all, so that together we may follow you and find the way home. Amen.

Each time we hear this text it is as though we stood in the field outside Bethlehem with the myriad stars in the sky above us. We feel something of what the philosopher felt, who never grew weary of the wonder of two things: the stars in the heavens above and the voice of conscience within.

As we examine this story in more detail we find that not only stars twinkle over our heads. We discover that there are many problems connected with this story, and they, too, are over our heads! Let us list a few of these problems.

The Wise Men

Who were they, these wise men, and where did they come from? In the history of the church they are covered with a golden net of legend. They were kings. And doesn't the prophet say that "nations shall come to your light, and kings to the brightness of your rising"? Legend has even named them: Caspar and Balthasar and Melchior.

In the text itself we find little justification for such conjectures. We merely learn that they were wise men or magi, as they are also called. From the story we may infer what sort of wisdom they were concerned with. It appears they dabbled in astrology, the study of the meaning of the stars. In olden days that was a reputable subject for study, although in our day it is only a more or less respectable source of income for magazines devoted to it. We don't know more than that about the wise men. All efforts at investigating their movements and motives have been in vain. They remain anonymous.

The Star

Our next question is this: What had the wise men actually seen which caused them to set out on their journey? "We have seen his star in the East," they said. Does that mean that they had seen it while they were in the East, or that they had seen it in the eastern heavens? The original Greek permits either interpretation, and even a third. The word "east" means "rising," so the meaning might be, "We have seen his star rise."

It is reasonable to believe that they actually were "wise men from the East." It was chiefly in the East, in the lands around the Tigris and Euphrates rivers, that astrology was practiced. And it would be on a journey from east to west that we can most easily imagine a star going before them to show them the way. As a matter of accuracy, however, considering the way the land lies, they must have travelled north a good deal of the time.

Even down to the present, many hypotheses have been advanced to explain what it was the wise men had really seen. It has been customary to assume that it was a constellation made up of two planets which drew their attention, rather than a single star. Likewise, people have tried to discover how the star led them, why the sight of the star caused them to think about a king in the land of the Jews, how the star guided them to the stable and remained fixed above it. Such conjectures serve to pass the time, but they are, after all, merely guesswork. Guesswork may be a sop to curiosity, but it is merely air and bubbles for those who are seeking bread for eternal life.

As a matter of fact, we could go through the

entire account and find more and more questions to ask. What actually happened? We ask, but the Gospel gives no answers. There is not much the evangelist knows, or at least tells us, about the wise men and their journey. They remain unknown representatives of all who approach the manger and the child by unknown ways. We become no wiser by turning to the other evangelists and Bible writers. Except for our text, there is not a single reference to our unknown friends and their wanderings in the whole of Scripture.

Yet, even if the account contains many unanswered and unanswerable questions, it does include the great, glittering star which no one can fail to see.

> In the midst of Christmas night,
> While the stars were shining bright.

Even though there were so many stars that we cannot distinguish one from the others,

> Of a sudden, clear and radiant,
> One appeared and shone resplendent
> With the luster of the sun.

A Message for All Mankind

We are left in no doubt as to what this story has to say to us. Its purpose is to make the great message of Christmas night come really alive: "Behold, I bring you good news of a great joy

which will come *to all the people.*" The story of
the wise men says to us that this is something
intended for *everybody.* It is not confined to the
people of Israel, to the people of our own land,
to the people of the early church; the Gospel pays
no attention to boundaries. It is the Gospel for
the world, the whole world. — *for each one of us here tonight —*

This means that these representatives of the *even for*
nameless and numberless hordes of heathens have *few / friedhe/*
something to say, not least to the Christianity of *all not here*
our day. We live in a world in which distances
have disappeared and boundaries are being oblit-
erated. People, nations, races and continents are
being hurled into the melting pot of history.
Everybody affects everybody else as never before.
We are thrust almost unpleasantly into one an-
others' lives. The time is gone when a people
could live safely behind its own hedge, joined in
a common culture, united by a time-honored view
of life, completely unmoved by the fact that other
peoples have other values and customs, even
other thoughts about life and death. Today we
are forced in upon one another, whether we are
black or white, red or yellow. We can no longer
pretend we are alone on this globe.

As a matter of fact, the church has always
known this, especially in those periods of its history when it has been most awakened and alive.
The church has always known that God loves all

mankind, and that witness to his love must be carried to the ends of the earth.

The sons and daughters of the church have gone out bearing the light to all the world. They have discovered humanity's oneness and have learned the duty of the rich to share what they have. They have done this even when the world's "wisdom" had nothing but sneers for those who "knitted woolen socks for Africa" and didn't seem to understand that the bushman was best off when we left him to himself while we occupied ourselves with the welfare of those at home.

The light of Christmas is for all. If it is to stream freely to us, we must let it stream freely to others. As soon as we try to keep it for ourselves, we lose it.

What, then, do we have to give to the world? Our western, so-called Christian, culture? Our splendid church and organizational structure? Our moral standards, our religious customs?

There may be values in our Christian, cultural and humane development which may be passed on advantageously. But none of this which we call our own, rightly or wrongly, is the true light. At most it is a reflection of the light, and not always the best reflection. The light is the miracle of Christmas, and that miracle took place before and without any connection with all our Chris-

tian gyrations. The light is *from* God, the light is
of God. He alone is its source.

Christianity must lose every feeling of superior-
ity. We cannot go to the peoples and nations of
the world in the conviction that we know it all
and that others must struggle up to the heights
we occupy. Even if we belong to a flock only a
few hundred yards away while they come from a
land hundreds of miles away, that does not mean
that we are at home while they are strangers when
we meet in the stable. Shepherds and wise men
are equally welcome there. Who dares to say that
the manger in which the child lies or the sheep
who daily eat at it are ours? Who on the other side
dares to boast, "We brought gold, frankincense
and myrrh. What did you bring? Grass and moss
and sheep manure!"

> In Christ there is no east or west,
> In him no south or north,
> But one great fellowship of love
> Throughout the whole wide earth.
> (SBH 342, stanza 1)

What blessed star is this which leads us here
where true unity is to be found, where spirits
meet and find one another? When we were children, we sang:

> In his Word did God provide
> Such a star to be our guide.
> Holy Writ, the Gospel story,
> Doth reveal to us the glory,
> Leading onward, on to Christ.

We do not know what drove our wise friends out on their wanderings. It is possible that they had heard of Israel's faith and hope, and it is also possible that they had learned from their Jewish neighbors about the Messiah who was to come. Many Jewish families lived in the cities and cultural centers of the East. Long before then the Holy Scriptures had been translated into Greek. The faith and hope of Israel were not unknown throughout the world.

But again we are dealing in conjectures! We do not know how the wise men became acquainted with the prophecies of the Bible. We do know from the story that they needed additional guidance from Scripture to tell them that they must go to Bethlehem. They were set on the right road by Bible scholars who were not interested themselves in finding the Savior but instead put their vast store of knowledge at the disposal of a worldly ruler who sought to take the life of the royal child. Yet, despite their blindness, God used even these scholars.

The Lord guards his Word and makes sure that he who honestly seeks guidance receives it. The one who turns to Scripture only to find theories and sidelights on all the interesting subjects in the world finds exactly that, and no more. But the one who seeks guidance and counsel and who is filled with the great question, "Where shall I seek

to find the royal child?"—that person finds what
he seeks. Blessed is the one who seeks earnestly!

The Search for Meaning in Life

Deep in God's creation lies an anticipation, a
longing, a question. Among all peoples and in all
cultures we can discern stirrings, unrest. The longing is universal to find meaning in life, to find a
place to kneel, to find a Master who deserves our
homage. The Creator has made that longing a
part of his creation. Wherever and whenever we
encounter that longing we should meet it with
honor and respect.

But our longing is always unclear and tinged
with romanticism and corrupted by dreams of
our own greatness. We lose sight of the star, we
let so many things obscure it. In the dark of the
night we lose our way; we confuse the light of
the star with the neon lights along the street.
Only when the Word has enlightened us, correct-
ed us, and put our feet back on the right course
can we see the star again.

We do not own the star. But it leads us if we
are willing to be led. When Christians bring their
great and glorious news to heathen at home and
abroad, they do not point to themselves or to the
Christian fellowship to which they belong. They
point away from themselves toward the light.

They point to him who is the Word, the Word which on Christmas night "became flesh and dwelt among us."

The Bible is a well of light, each ray streaming out from the same center: the child in the manger, God with us. As a historical and human document it may be imperfect, but it is one hundred per cent dependable as the guide for those who seek the child of the King.

Our Lord and God has never promised full knowledge to the one who seeks in the Bible for information concerning distant things and forgotten times, or for knowledge concerning the makeup of the world and the course of nature. But he who seeks the Word in the words, the child in the book, the king in the manger, will never be led astray.

With this star as our guide, with this glory as our hope, we stretch out our arms to the world and say, "Come with us to the stable, to the true center of the world, to the gathering place of the human race." There shines the star—no one owns it alone. Amen.